# PINUP GIRLS

# A SEXY COLORING BOOK FOR ADULTS

# MORE OUR BOOKS : http://bit.ly/vart_page

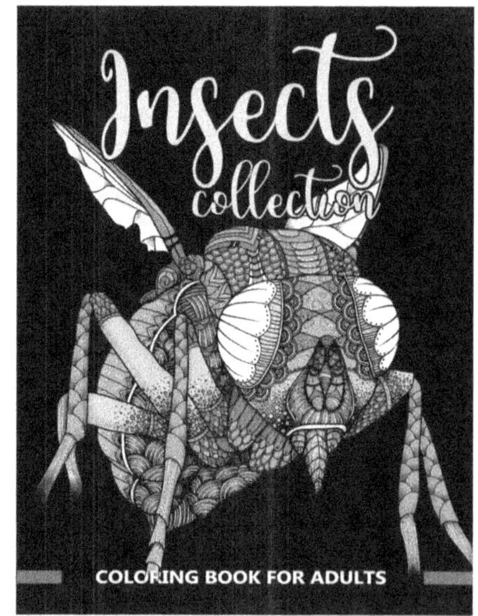

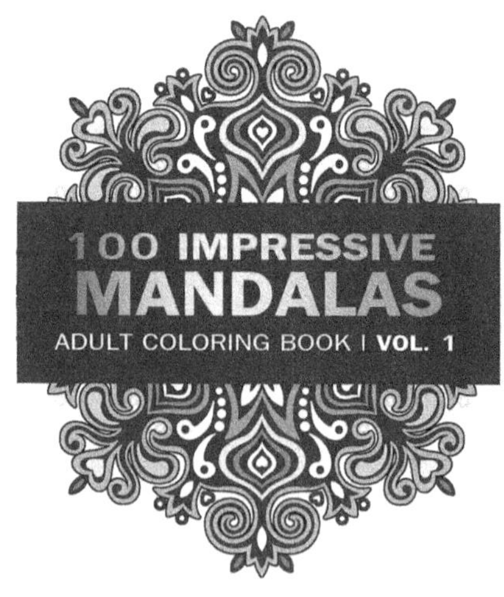

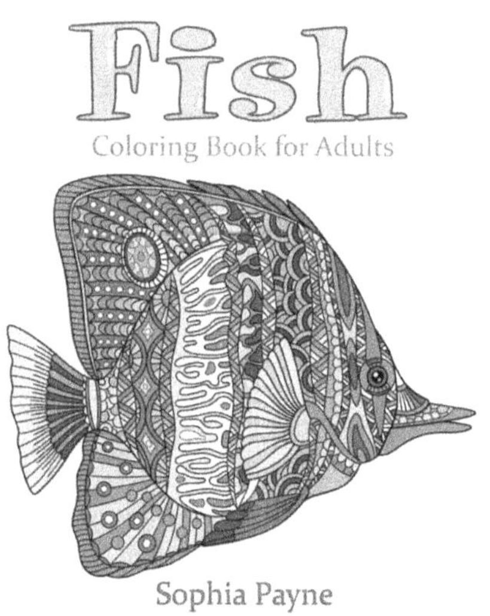

BACKYARD
PARTY

# GET FREE OUR COLORING PAGES and Promotion Update

## At : bit.ly/get_gift_coloring

## Insects Collection Coloring Book

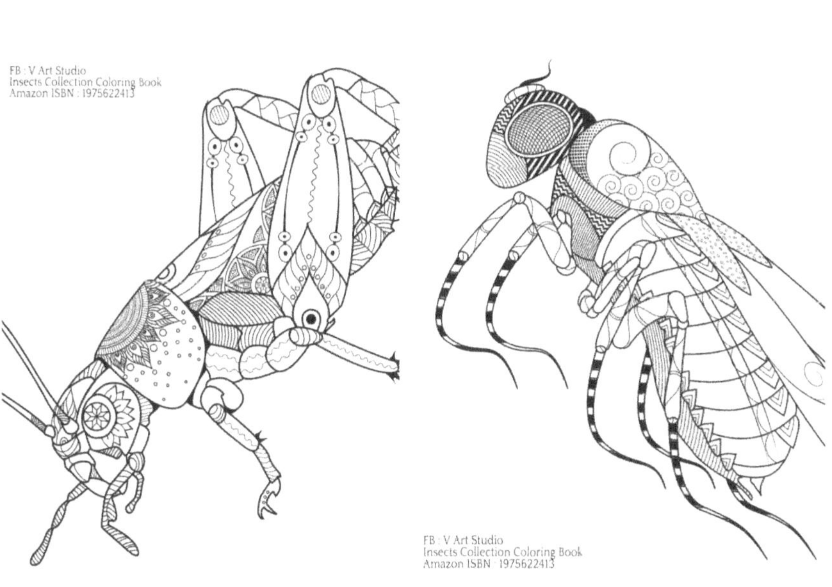

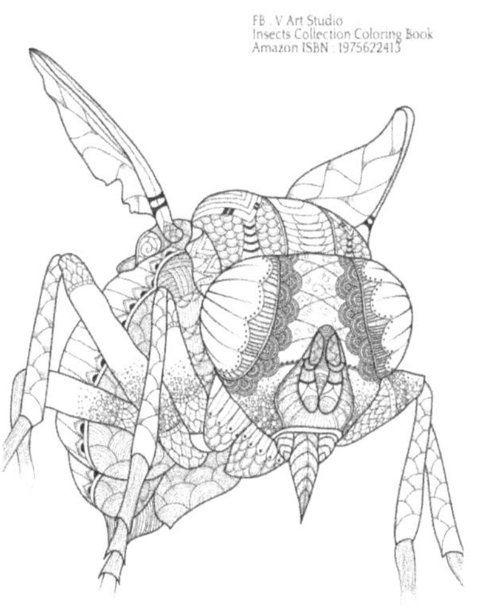

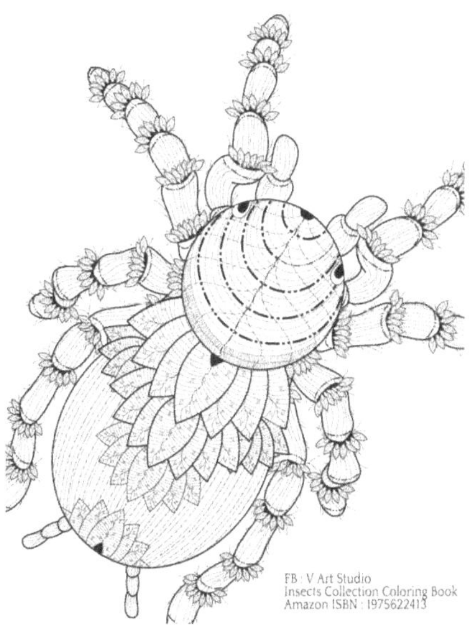

*Your Amazon Review could really help us.
Thank you for your support.*